YOUR ANCIENT
EGYPT

Homework Helper

by *Anita Ganeri*
Consultant: Dr. Anne Millard

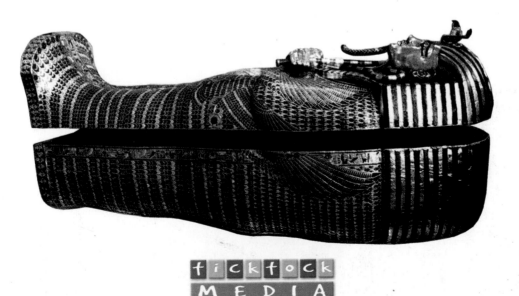

ticktock
MEDIA

How to use this book

Each topic in this book is clearly labelled and contains all these components:

Topic heading

Introduction to the topic

Sub-topic 1 offers complete information about one aspect of the topic

Choose a word from the Keyword Contents on page 3. Then, turn to the correct page and look for your word in BOLD CAPITALS. This will take you straight to the information you need

Mummies

Words to use in your project
anthropoid
corpse (dead
dessicated (

For a dead person's soul to survive and prosper in the Next World, the Egyptians believed that the person's BODY must be preserved and not allowed to rot away. They went to great lengths to make sure that this happened. To stop bodies from decaying, they developed a process called mummification. This was so successful that archaeologists have found many mummies which have survived surprisingly intact.

HOW MUMMIES WERE MADE

We know about how mummies were made from pictures in tombs and coffins and from the writings of the ancient Greek historian, Herodotus. He visited Egypt in the 5th century BC. This is what his evidence tells us:

1. First the embalmers washed the body of the dead person.

2. The **BRAIN** was pulled out through the nose with an iron hook.

3. A slit was cut in the left side of the body and the liver, lungs, stomach and intestines were taken out. They were placed in four stone containers, called canopic jars. The **HEART** was left in place.

4. The body was cleaned out and packed with 'natron', a salty chemical. Then it was left for 40 days for the natron to dry it out.

5. When the body was dry, it was stuffed with sawdust or cloth, natron and sweet-smelling herbs. The skin was rubbed with ointment and coated in resin.

6. Then it was wrapped in linen **BANDAGES** with amulets and jewellery placed between the layers.

7. Sometimes a painted **MASK** was put over the mummy's head. Finally, the mummy was placed in a coffin, to start its journey through the afterlife.

Source – Herodotus, Histories II, c. 480–429 BC

COFFINS

The earliest **COFFINS** were plain baskets or wooden boxes, later coffins became much more ornate. Royal coffins were even covered with gold and semi-precious stones. Human-shaped coffins came into use in about 2,000 BC, and stayed in fashion for over 2,000 years. During the Middle Kingdom private coffins contained pictures of gods and

This coffin is made of gold-covered crimson glass and blue pottery.

Source – The Egyptian Book of the Dead, New Kingdom

Mummies Glossary

amulets	*Lucky charms*	mum
archaeologist	*Person who digs things up to study history*	
canopic jars	*Containers in which a dead person's lungs, liver, stomach were kept*	natr papy
embalmers	*People who did the mummification*	resir
preserved	*Kept for a long time*	sarce

See also: Pharaohs 6–7; Religion 10–11; Pyramids and Tombs 14–15; F

The Glossary explains the meaning of any unusual or difficult words appearing on these two pages

Copyright © *ticktock* Entertainment Ltd 2004
First published in Great Britain in 2004 by *ticktock* Media Ltd.,
Unit 2, Orchard Business Centre, North Farm Road, Tunbridge Wells, Kent, TN2 3XF
We would like to thank: Egan-Reid Ltd for their help with this book.
ISBN 1 86007 538 X HB
ISBN 1 86007 532 0 PB
Printed in China
A CIP catalogue record for this book is available from the British Library.

Sub-topic 2 offers complete information about one aspect of the topic

Some suggested words to use in your project

The Case Study is a closer look at a famous person, artefact or building that relates to the topic

cavated (dug up) purified (cleaned)
grant (sweet-smelling) swathed (wrapped)
celess (very valuable) ornate (decorative)

Each photo or illustration is described and discussed in its accompanying text

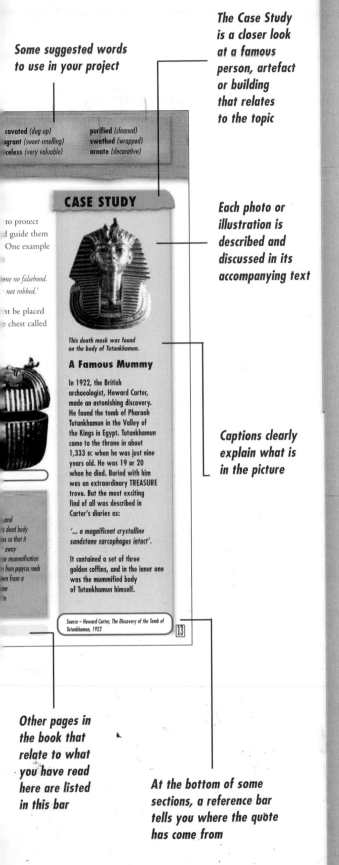

to protect
d guide them
One example

me no falsehood.
not robbed.'

t be placed
chest called

CASE STUDY

This death mask was found on the body of Tutankhamun.

A Famous Mummy

In 1922, the British archaeologist, Howard Carter, made an astonishing discovery. He found the tomb of Pharaoh Tutankhamun in the Valley of the Kings in Egypt. Tutankhamun came to the throne in about 1,333 BC when he was just nine years old. He was 19 or 20 when he died. Buried with him was an extraordinary TREASURE trove. But the most exciting find of all was described in Carter's diaries as:

'... a magnificent crystalline sandstone sarcophagus intact'.

It contained a set of three golden coffins, and in the inner one was the mummified body of Tutankhamun himself.

and
dead body
es so that it
away
or mummification
from papyrus reeds
m from a
ee
n

Captions clearly explain what is in the picture

Source – Howard Carter, The Discovery of the Tomb of Tutankhamun, 1922

13

Other pages in the book that relate to what you have read here are listed in this bar

At the bottom of some sections, a reference bar tells you where the quote has come from

Keyword Contents

The Land of Egypt

The CIVILISATION of ancient Egypt was one of the earliest and greatest in the world. It grew up along the banks of the River Nile more than 7,000 years ago, and lasted for more than 3,000 years. The first SETTLERS were probably people who had escaped the droughts of Africa by coming to Egypt. They began to build villages of mud huts and to grow crops and domesticate cattle.

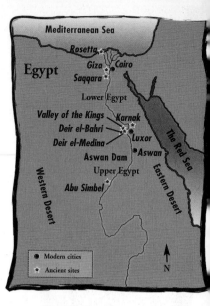

FIRST DISCOVERIES

For hundreds of years, the SECRETS of ancient Egypt were not known.

Then, in 1822, a French man named Jean Francois Champollion managed to **TRANSLATE** the Egyptian system of writing, called hieroglyphics. Many ancient temples, tombs, pyramids and cities were also explored around this time. These had been remarkably well preserved by the dry desert heat. The tombs, in particular, proved to be rich sources of information as their walls were decorated with scenes of daily life and religious practices. Also, people were often buried with their possessions – including jewellery, furniture, household objects and even clothes and food. From these, experts were able to piece together a fascinating picture of life in ancient Egypt.

We know much about the daily life of ancient Egyptians from tomb paintings like this one from about 1,250 BC at the Sennedjem tomb in Thebes.

Words to use in your project

archaeologists (people who study history by digging up the past)
artefacts (ancient objects)
Egyptology (study of ancient Egypt)
evidence (proof)
excavated (dug up)
mythology (set of beliefs)
pharaohs (Egyptian kings)
preserved (kept intact)

RULED BY KINGS

Over time, the villages of ancient Egypt grew to become towns and cities, and eventually formed two **KINGDOMS** – Upper Egypt in the Nile Valley and Lower Egypt in the Nile Delta. Archaeologists think that King Menes of Upper Egypt united the two kingdoms around 3,100 BC. The unity of the two kingdoms was symbolised by the double **CROWN** of Upper and Lower Egypt. The Greek writer Herodotus (b. 490 BC), who visited Egypt, wrote an account of the life and history of the country from talking to priests. His writings tell us that Menes built a new capital at Memphis:

'When this Min (Menes), who first became King, had made into dry land the part which was dammed off, he founded in it that city which is now called Memphis ... Then secondly he established in the city the temple of Hephaistes, a great work and worthy of mention.'

This is a statue of Pharaoh Ramses II wearing the double crown of Upper and Lower Egypt.

Source – Herodotus, Histories II, c. 480–c.429 BC

The Land of Egypt Glossary

civilisation	A culture and its people	**inexhaustible**	Never gets tired
delta	Pile of sediment at the mouth of a river	**pharaoh**	Egyptian king
		pyramids	Triangular-shaped Egyptian tombs
domesticate	Taming animals		
Hephaistes	Greek god of craftsmen	**Ra**	Egyptian sun god
hieroglyphics	The Egyptian system of picture writing	**tombs**	Where dead bodies are buried

CASE STUDY

The River Nile was vital for life to prosper in the deserts of Egypt.

The River Nile

More than 90 percent of Egypt is covered in hot, dry **DESERT** where very little can grow. The ancient Egyptians called it 'the Red Land'. They lived on narrow strips of land on either side of the **RIVER NILE**. Egypt's wealth was based on farming and, without the river, it would not have been successful. The importance of the Nile is revealed in an ancient poem called the 'Hymn to the Nile':

'Hail to thee, O Nile! Who manifests thyself over this land, and comes to give life to Egypt! Watering the orchards – created by Ra, to cause all the cattle to live, you give the earth to drink, inexhaustible one.'

Source – Hymn to the Nile, c. 2,000 BC

See also: Pharaohs 6–7; Language and Writing 8–9; Religion 10–11; Farming 18–19

Pharaohs

Ancient Egypt was ruled by KINGS who were believed to be the god Horus in human form. The king was thought to be so holy that it was disrepectful to call him directly by name. Instead, he was given the title of 'pharaoh' which means 'great house' or 'palace'. The pharaoh was head of the government, kept LAW AND ORDER, led the army and controlled trade and industry.

AKHENATEN & NEFERTITI

Akhenaten ruled ancient Egypt from about 1,364–1,347 BC. He was married to Nefertiti who may have been his co-ruler for a while.

We know a lot about life during Akhenaten and Nefertiti's reign from the contents of the Amarna letters discovered in 1887. These were letters sent to Akhenaten by kings and officials from different parts of the Middle East. One tells how parts of the Empire felt neglected by the Pharoah:

'And now your city weeps, and her tears are running, and there is no hope for us. For 20 years we have been sending to our lord, the King of Egypt, but there is not come to us a word, not one...'

Another tells of a **PLOT** against Akhenaten:

'You must know that Shipt-Ba'ad and Zimrida are conspiring... Now I have sent you Raphae-el. He will bring the Great Man intelligence concerning the matter.'

This painted limestone statue of King Akhenaten and Queen Nefertiti was found at Tell el-Amarna.

Source – Amarna Letters, 14th century BC. You can read the Amarna letters at: http://nefertiti.iwebland.com/amarnaletters.htm

Words to use in your project

correspondence (letters)	monarch (ruler)	regal (royal)
dynasty (line of kings)	officials (people with	successor (next in line to
legacy (passed on)	important duties)	the throne)

WOMAN RULERS

There were very few **WOMAN RULERS** in ancient Egypt. The most remarkable of these was Queen Hatshepsut who ruled from about 1,490– 1,468 BC. Throughout her reign, Hatshepsut was addressed as 'His Majesty' and sculptures often show her dressed as a man and wearing the ceremonial royal beard. She had a tomb in the Valley of the Kings and a beautiful funeral tomb at Deir el-Bahiri. She boasted that she restored temples destroyed by earlier foreign invaders:

'I have raised up what was dismembered even from the first time when the Asiatics were in the North Land.'

One of Egypts most famous queens (who may have co-ruled with her husband Akhenaten) was Nefertiti who was admired for her great beauty. A sculptured head of Nefertiti was found at Amarna. The last pharaoh to ever reign in Egypt was Cleopatra who was actually of Greek descent.

Queen Hatshepsut was the most powerful female pharaoh. This statue stands at the side of Hatshepsut's temple in Deir el-Bahri.

Source – Inscription on Hatshepsut's temple at Speos Artemidos, c. 1,490 BC

See also: Religion 10–11; Pyramids and Tombs 14–15; Priests and Temples 16–17; War and Weapons 24–25

CASE STUDY

Many statues of Pharaoh Ramesses II still stand today, such as this one at Luxor.

Ramesses the Great

One of the best-known kings of Egypt, Ramesses II (or Ramesses the Great) ruled from about 1,289–1,224 BC. During his long reign, he had more temples, statues and **MONUMENTS** built to honour the gods than any other pharaoh. Ramesses also led the Egyptian army in the Battle of Kadesh against the Hittites – the Egyptians' greatest enemies. Eventually the two sides made peace. Descriptions of Ramesses' army have been found carved onto walls:

'... [covering] the mountains and the valleys; they were like grasshoppers in their multitudes'.

Source – The Poem of Pentaur, c. 1,290 BC

Pharaohs Glossary

ceremonial	Used during special ceremonies		a single king or queen	multitudes	Masses
conspiring	Making secret plans	Hittites	Ancient civilisation from Anatolia	neglected	Fail to give proper care or
descent	Person's origin or nationality		(modern-day Turkey)		attention to something
dismembered	Divided up	Horus	The Egyptian god of the sky	pharaoh	Ruler in ancient Egypt
empire	Group of states ruled over by	intelligence	Secret information	reign	Rule as a king or queen

Language and Writing

The ancient Egyptians were among the earliest people to write things down in around 3,500 BC. To do this, the Egyptians invented a script called HIEROGLYPHICS in which each hieroglyph, or picture, stood for an object or idea. The word 'hieroglyph' was invented by the ancient Greeks, and means 'sacred carving'. For the Egyptians, writing was sacred. They believed that the skill had been given to them by the god of wisdom, Thoth.

HOW HIEROGLYPHICS WORKED

There were over 700 hieroglyphyic signs. Many of these were PICTURES of people, animals and objects.

The main Egyptian system of writing was called hieroglyphics and used pictures to represent ideas.

Each sign could represent an object or stand for the sound of one or more letters. Hieroglyphs were normally consonants. In order to say a word, vowels had to be added. There were many different ways of writing hieroglyphs – from left to right, right to left, or top to bottom. If the signs for animals or people faced left, they were read from left to right. If they faced right, they were read from right to left. Hieroglyphs were used for important inscriptions on temples, tombs and official records. The Egyptians used a much simpler and quicker script called hieratic for business, story-writing and religious documents.

Words to use in your project

breakthrough *(great success)*
communication *(sharing information)*

decipher *(decode)*
documents *(official papers)*
palette *(a box containing inks*

and brushes)
represent *(stand for)*
scholar *(expert)*

SCRIBES

Hieroglyphs were very complicated. Professional **WRITERS**, called scribes, had to be trained at special schools. The training began when a boy was about nine years old, and took seven to 12 years to complete. Once the students were good enough, they were allowed to write on papyrus **SCROLLS** using reed pens dipped in red or black **INK**. Good scribes might get a job in a temple, the law court or the government or travel with the army to write battle reports. One text had this advice for pupils:

'Apply yourself to this noble profession. You will be advanced by your superiors. Love writing, shun dancing, do not long for the marsh thicket. By day write with your fingers; recite by night. Befriend the scroll ... it pleases more than wine.'

Scribes were usually shown sitting cross-legged and holding their writing materials like this statue from a tomb at Saqqara.

Source – Papyrus Lansing, Late-New Kingdom

Language and Writing Glossary

demotic	*Egyptian shorthand script*	**New Kingdom**	*Name given to united Upper and Lower Kingdoms*
hieratic	*Simple style of writing used in everyday life*	**papyrus**	*A paper-like material made from reeds*
hieroglyphs	*Ancient Egyptian style of writing using pictures*	**scribe**	*A professional writer*
inscription	*Words written on paper, stone or metal*	**script**	*The signs or letters used to write a language down*

CASE STUDY

The discovery of the Rosetta Stone in 1,799 BC meant that the ancient Egyptian language could finally be translated.

The Rosetta Stone

When ancient Egypt was conquered by Rome more than 2,000 years ago, the art of reading and writing hieroglyphs gradually died out. Then, in 1799, a soldier in Napoleon Bonaparte's army made a thrilling **DISCOVERY** in Rosetta, Egypt. He found a large, stone slab covered in ancient writing. On the stone, the same text was written out in three different scripts – hieroglyphic, demotic (a simpler Egyptian script) and Greek. A Frenchman named Jean Francois Champollion knew Greek and compared the other two scripts to it. By doing this, he was finally able to crack the **CODE** and solve the mystery of the hieroglyphs.

Source – Jean Francois Champollion, Egyptian Diaries: A Voyage to the Mysteries of Egypt, 1928–9

See also: The Land of Egypt 4–5; Work and Play 20–21; War and Weapons 24–25; Families 28–29

Religion

The ancient Egyptians worshipped dozens of GODS AND GODDESSES. They were believed to rule the natural world and control all aspects of daily life. Some gods and goddesses were worshipped throughout Egypt. Others were special to particular cities or towns.

THE SUN GOD

One of the most important gods in Egyptian religion was Ra the sun god. He had many different forms and names and sometimes appears as a man with a hawk's head on a sun disc surrounded by a cobra.

Ra was believed to have created the world and everything in it. According to Egyptian mythology, he set sail across the **HEAVENS** every morning in a boat. At night, Ra sailed through the **UNDERWORLD**, bringing light to the dead and leaving the world in darkness, rising again every morning. Later, Ra merged with the god, Amun, to become Amun-Ra, king of the gods. The Egyptian *Book of the Dead* tells us of Ra's importance:

'The gods rejoice when they see Ra crowned upon his throne, and when his beams flood the world with light ... May Ra give glory, and power, and truth-speaking ... Hail you gods of the house of the soul, who ... give celestial food to the dead.'

This is Horus, the falcon-headed god of the sky. He was the guardian of the king and the son of Isis and Osiris.

Source – 'A Hymn of Praise to Ra when he rises in the eastern part of Heaven', Egyptian Book of the Dead, New Kingdom

Words to use in your project

cemetery *(burial ground)*
deity *(god or goddess)*
inscription *(carved words)*

judgement *(judged by god)*
reincarnation *(being born again)*

soul *(spirit of a person that lives on past death)*
spiritual *(religious)*

LIFE AFTER DEATH

The Egyptians believed in **LIFE AFTER DEATH** and called it the Next World. But for a person's soul to enter the Next World, it had to go through a series of trials in the Underworld. If it passed these, it entered the Judgement Hall of Osiris, ruler of the dead. There it first had to recite the 'Negative Confession' which included the following promises:

'I have not committed sin ... I have not commited robbery with violence ... I have not stolen ... I have not uttered curses ... I have not uttered lies ... I have not been angry without just cause ... I have not eaten the heart ... I have not slandered any man ... I have terrorized none.'

The Judgment Hall of Osiris was where dead souls were tested to see whether they had led a good or bad life.

There are many Egyptian gods and goddesses. Here are some of the more common ones:

Isis	mother goddess
Maat	goddess of truth and justice
Osiris	god of the underworld
Ra	sun god
Thoth	moon god
Hathor	goddess of love
Ptah	god of craftsmen

> Source – 'The Negative Confession', Egyptian Book of the Dead, New Kingdom

Religion Glossary

avenger	Person who seeks revenge	slandered	Something said that damages a person's reputation
celestial	To do with Heaven or the stars	sovereign	Supreme ruler
mummified	The Egyptian way of embalming a body and wrapping it in bandages	terrorized	Threatened and scared
		Underworld	Home for the dead according to Egyptian mythology
sacred	Holy		

See also: Pharaohs 6–7; Mummies 12–13; Pyramids and Tombs 14–15; Priests and Temples 16–17

CASE STUDY

Sacred Cats

Certain animals such as **CATS**, bulls and the ibis bird were considered sacred by the Egyptians. They were believed to be earthly forms of the gods. When cats died, they were mummified and some were put in cat-shaped coffins. Then, they were sold to temple visitors who could bury them in the temple cemetery as an offering to the goddess, Bastet. Another important cat protected the god, Ra. An inscription on a tombs at Thebes reads:

'Thou art the Great Cat, the avenger of the gods, and the judge of words, and the president of the sovereign chiefs and the governor of the holy Circle; thou art indeed ... the Great Cat.'

Anyone who deliberately killed a cat could be sentenced to death.

Many cat statues have been found in tombs like this one from Saqqara, dating from about 600 BC.

> Source – Inscription on the Royal Tombs at Thebes, New Kingdom

Mummies

For a dead person's soul to survive and prosper in the Next World, the Egyptians believed that the person's BODY must be preserved and not allowed to rot away. They went to great lengths to make sure that this happened. To stop bodies from decaying, they developed a process called mummification. This was so successful that archaeologists have found many mummies which have survived surprisingly intact.

HOW MUMMIES WERE MADE

We know about how mummies were made from pictures in tombs and coffins and from the writings of the ancient Greek historian, Herodotus. He visited Egypt in the 5th century BC. This is what his evidence tells us:

1. First the embalmers washed the body of the dead person.

2. The **BRAIN** was pulled out through the nose with an iron hook.

3. A slit was cut in the left side of the body and the liver, lungs, stomach and intestines were taken out. They were placed in four stone containers, called 'canopic jars'. The **HEART** was left in place.

4. The body was cleaned out and packed with 'natron', a salty chemical. Then it was left for 40 days for the natron to dry it out.

5. When the body was dry, it was stuffed with sawdust or cloth, natron and sweet-smelling herbs. The skin was rubbed with ointment and coated in resin.

6. Then it was wrapped in linen **BANDAGES** with amulets and jewellery placed between the layers.

7. Sometimes a painted **MASK** was put over the mummy's head. Finally, the mummy was placed in a coffin, to start its journey through the afterlife.

Source – Herodotus, Histories II, c. 480–429 BC

COFFINS

The earliest **COFFINS** were plain baskets or wooden boxes, later coffins became much more ornate. Royal coffins were even covered with gold and semi-precious stones. Human-shaped coffins came into use in about 2,000 BC, and stayed in fashion for over 2,000 years. During the Middle Kingdom private coffins contained pictures of gods and spells on the coffin to protect the dead person and guide them to the Next World. One example of such a spell read:

'Oh far strider, I have done no falsehood. Oh fire-embracer, I have not robbed.'

Several coffins might be placed inside a large, stone chest called a sarcophagus.

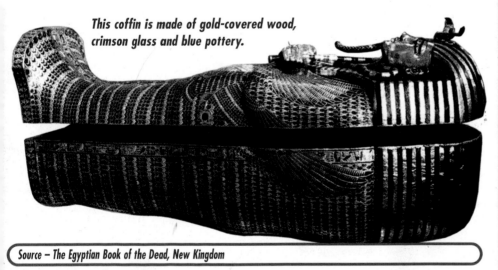

This coffin is made of gold-covered wood, crimson glass and blue pottery.

Source – The Egyptian Book of the Dead, New Kingdom

Mummies Glossary

amulets	*Lucky charms*	mummification	*Preserving and*
archaeologist	*Person who digs things up to study history*		*wrapping a dead body in bandages so that it doesn't rot away*
canopic jars	*Containers in which a dead person's lungs, liver, stomach were kept*	natron	*Salt used for mummification*
		papyruses	*Scrolls made from papyrus reeds*
embalmers	*People who did the mummification*	resin	*A sticky gum from a plant or tree*
preserved	*Kept for a long time*	sarcophagus	*Stone coffin*

See also: Pharaohs 6–7; Religion 10–11; Pyramids and Tombs 14–15; Priests and Temples 16–17

CASE STUDY

This death mask was found on the body of Tutankhamun.

A Famous Mummy

In 1922, the British archaeologist, Howard Carter, made an astonishing discovery. He found the tomb of Pharaoh Tutankhamun in the Valley of the Kings in Egypt. Tutankhamun came to the throne in about 1,333 BC when he was just nine years old. He was 19 or 20 when he died. Buried with him was an extraordinary **TREASURE** trove. But the most exciting find of all was described in Carter's diaries as:

'... a magnificent crystalline sandstone sarcophagus intact'.

It contained a set of three golden coffins, and in the inner one was the mummified body of Tutankhamun himself.

Source – Howard Carter, The Discovery of the Tomb of Tutankhamun, 1922

Pyramids and Tombs

To make sure that their bodies were preserved for ever, the Egyptian pharaohs had huge tombs built for themselves. Here, they hoped that they and the PRECIOUS THINGS they were taking with them into the Next World would be safe. The first pyramid was built as a tomb for King Djoser in about 2,630 BC. It had stepped sides which represented a giant stairway so that the king's soul could climb to Heaven. Later, pyramids were built with straight sides to symbolise the sun's rays.

HOW TO BUILD A PYRAMID

Historians think that the pyramids were built like this:

1. Teams of builders used wooden sledges to drag stone blocks into position.

2. The blocks were pulled up a ramp made of brick and mud.

Much of what we know about how the pyramids were made comes from excavations. The Greek writer, Herodotus, described the tomb BUILDERS at the Great Pyramid of Giza:

'The stones were quarried in the Arabian mountains and dragged to the Nile. They were carried across the river in boats and then dragged up the slope to the site of the pyramid ... They worked in gangs of 100,000 men, each gang for three months. The pyramid itself was 20 years in the making.'

Despite Herodotus' claim, scholars today believe that only 20,000 men were involved in the building of the pyramid.

Source – Herodotus, Histories II, c. 480–429 BC

Words to use in your project

adorned *(decorated)*
architect *(person who designs buildings)*

constructed *(built)*
implements *(tools)*
labour *(work)*

looted *(robbed)*
majestic *(grand)*
monument *(building)*

THE VALLEY OF THE KINGS

Later pharaohs chose to be buried in tombs cut deep into the cliff face in the Valley of the Kings, a remote valley on the edge of the desert to the west of the city of Thebes. Inside, they were decorated with scenes from the Next World. Non-royal tombs were **DECORATED** with wonderful scenes of daily life. Both royal and non-royal tombs were filled with treasure and so became a target for **ROBBERS**. The problem of grave-robbers is reflected in the poplular tale *Ali Baba and the 40 Thieves*:

Many pharaohs were buried in the Valley of the Kings in Thebes.

'*... when the chamber was finished, the king stored his money in it ... but when upon his opening the chamber a second and a third time the money was each time seen to be diminished, for the thieves did not slacken in their assaults against it ... having ordered traps to be made he set these round about the vessels in which the money was; ... now when it became day, the king entered into the chamber and was very greatly amazed, seeing the body of the thief held in the trap without his head...*'

Source – Herodotus, Histories II, c. 480–429 BC

Pyramids and Tombs Glossary

assaults	*Attacks*	**sarcophagus**	*A stone chest in which bodies are buried*
diminished	*Become less than*		
excavations	*Digging to find ancient buried remains*	**symbolise**	*To stand for; have a special meaning*
quarried	*Sourcing precious stones or minerals*	**tomb**	*A place where a dead person's body is buried*

CASE STUDY

The Great Pyramid

The largest pyramid, and one of the seven wonders of the ancient world, is the Great Pyramid of Giza. According to the writings of Manetho and Herodotus, it was built for King Khufu about 4,500 years ago. It stands about 146 metres tall and contains about 3,200,000 blocks of limestone, each weighing about 2.5 tonnes. The king's mummified body was buried in a stone sarcophagus in the King's Burial Chamber, deep inside the pyramid. In the Middle Kingdom, pharaohs had false passages and **SECRET ENTRANCES** added to put off tomb-robbers tempted to steal the treasures buried with the king. Despite these efforts, treasures were still stolen.

The Great Pyramid of Giza was the tallest building in the world for nearly 4,500 years.

Explore the Great Pyramid on the Internet at:
http://www.pbs.org/wgbh/nova/pyramid/explore/khufu.html

Priests and Temples

Egyptian temples were dedicated to a particular god or goddess. They were believed to be the gods' homes on Earth. Only priests and priestesses were allowed to go inside the temples to WORSHIP. Ordinary Egyptians could only go as far as the temple entrance or the courtyard to say PRAYERS and to leave offerings for the gods. As chief priest, the pharaoh could not be expected to visit every temple in Egypt, so he appointed priests to perform the ceremonies for him.

TEMPLES

Studying archaeological remains and art tell us that a typical Egyptian temple followed this form:

• It was surrounded by an outer wall (A) containing a pylon, or temple gateway (B), that led into the temple enclosure.

• The temple proper had a pylon which was often flanked by two needle-shaped monuments, called obelisks, which were dedicated to the sun god.
• Inside, were one or more spacious courtyards (C).
• Next came the hall of columns (D) which would have been lavishly decorated with reliefs and columns.
• Right at the back was the sanctuary (E) – the most HOLY part of the temple. It contained the shrine in which the statue of the temple god or goddess was kept.

The Egyptians celebrated many annual festivals in honour of the gods and goddesses. On these special days, people were allowed inside the temples to celebrate. One example was the 'Beautiful Festival of the Valley' when people dressed in their best clothes and visited dead loved ones' tombs. We know the days the Egyptians celebrated festivals because many calendar dates were inscribed on temple walls.

Source – Temple of Ramesses III at Medinet Habu, c. 1,180 BC

Words to use in your project

ceremonies *(formal occasions)*
festival *(special day to be celebrated)*
performing *(acting)*
pious *(very religious)*
procession *(parade)*
religious *(believing in god or gods)*
worshipping *(honoruing gods)*

PRIESTS

Each temple had priests attached to it. Besides performing **RITUALS**, priests supervised the temple industries which included baking, brewing beer and tending the temple's lands. Priests were paid with a share of the food offered daily at the temple. A priest described his duties in preparing a body for burial:

'I decked the body of the lord of Abydos with ... every costly stone, among the ornaments of the limbs of a god. I dressed the god in his regalia by virtue of my office as master of secret things, and of my duty as priest.'

Priests could also become very wealthy. The writer Homer described how the priesthood at Thebes became very rich:

'The heaps of precious ingots gleam, the hundred-gated Thebes.'

This statue of a priest from about 2,650 BC features an inscription which names the first three kings of the 2nd dynasty.

Source – The Ikhernofret Stela c. 1,860 BC; and The Iliad, Book 9, c. 700 BC

CASE STUDY

Temple of Luxor

The Temple of Luxor was built by Pharaoh Amenhotep III with later additions built by other pharaohs such as Ramesses II. The temple was dedicated to the god Amun-Ra and was built in Thebes close to the River Nile. The temple is 850 feet long and 213 feet across in the front. In ancient times a 2-mile long avenue of **SPHINXES** connected the temple to the Temple of Karnak. The great **FESTIVAL** celebrated at Luxor was the Festival of Opet where the **SACRED** statue of Amun was taken on a procession by land and river from Karnak to Luxor.

Two long lines of sphinxes once stretched all the way from Luxor to Karnak. Some of the sphinxes are still standing.

Priests and Temples Glossary

decked	Decorated or dressed		a religious ceremony
ingot	Block of gold	**sanctuary**	The holiest part of a temple
ornaments	Decorative objects	**sphinx**	Ancient Egyptian stone figure
regalia	Objects that symbolise royalty		featuring lion's body and
ritual	Actions performed during		human head

See also: See also: Pharoahs 6–7; Religion 10–11; Pyramids and Tombs 14–15; Work and Play 20–21

Farming

Many ancient Egyptians worked as farmers along the River Nile. Most people did not own their own land. Instead, they farmed land on large estates that belonged to wealthy government officials or temples. Farmers kept part of their crops for themselves, but each year, they had to pay tax to the LANDOWNER and to the pharaoh. They were punished if they failed to do this. The Egyptian farming year was divided into three seasons.

GROWING AND HARVESTING

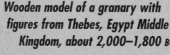

Wooden model of a granary with figures from Thebes, Egypt Middle Kingdom, about 2,000–1,800 BC.

Scenes painted in tombs across Egypt and small models found in tombs tell us much about Egyptian farming.

The growing season started in November, when the farmers ploughed the land and sowed the **SEEDS**. The **HARVEST** season began in March, done by hand, using wooden and flint sickles. Then, the grain was taken to the threshing floor where cattle trampled it to separate the grain from the stalks. Next, the grain and husks were separated, and the grain was then kept in storehouses called granaries until it was required. Models of these granaries (see left) suggest bread was made here as well. Farmers worked very hard, as described in this account by the scribe Nebmare-nakht:

'By day he cuts his farming tools; by night he twists rope. Even his midday hour he spends on farm labor.'

Source – Nebmare-nakht, 12th century BC

CROPS AND ANIMALS

Wheat and barley were important crops for Egyptian farmers.

Texts and actual dried remains of plants from ancient Egypt tell us much about the crops they planted. The most common crops appear to have been BARLEY and WHEAT. Wheat was used for making bread and barley for making beer. Vegetables such as onions, garlic, lentils, beans and lettuces were also grown, as well as grapes for making wine. The bones of cattle, pigs, sheep and goats that date from the period have also been found by archaeologists. Egypt's harsh climate had a huge impact on the farmer's yield. An ancient text has been found where one angry farmer faces this problem:

'Now, what do you mean by having Sihathor coming to me with old, dried-out, northern barley from Memphis, instead of giving me ten sacks of good, new barley?'

Source – Hekanakhte and his angry letters, c. 2000 BC

Farming Glossary

fertile	Land that is good for farming	nilometer	Structure for measuring water levels
granaries	Buildings for storing grain		
husks	The dry outer covering of fruits and seeds	sickle	A sharp, hook-shaped tool for cutting grain
inundation	Another word for a flood	threshing	To beat the grain in order to separate the grain from the stalks
Middle Kingdom	Name given to Egypt between 2,055–1,650 BC	yield	Extent of crop growth

See also: The Land of Egypt 4–5; Work and Play 20–21; Trade and Transport 22–23; At Home 26–27

CASE STUDY

Nilometers were built to measure the River Nile during Flood season.

The Flood

The **FLOOD** season, or inundation, started in July. This was when the River Nile overflowed and flooded its banks, spreading black soil on the fields. While the fields were underwater, work came to a halt. This was the time of year when many farmers were called up to help with building royal tombs. The writer Herodotus records the importance of the annual floods:

'It is certain that now they gather in fruit from the earth with less labour than any other men ... the river has come up of itself and watered their fields.'

Source – Herodotus, Histories II, c. 480–429 BC

Work and Play

While most Egyptians worked as farmers and builders, if a man was well-educated, he might get a JOB as a scribe, priest, or government official. Skilled craftsmen were always in demand for making essential everyday items, like pots, baskets and sandals. Women were expected to tend to domestic duties. In their spare time, Egyptians marked religious festivals with music and dancing. Wrestling and hunting were favourite SPORTS.

ROYAL TOMB BUILDERS

The ARTISTS and CRAFTSMEN who worked on the royal tombs in the Valley of the Kings lived in a specially-built village called Deir el-Medina.

From their writings, we find out a great deal about the way they worked. The 60 or so workmen were divided into two gangs, each led by a foreman who was in charge. Just as important as the people who constructed the tombs were those who decorated the inside walls with paintings and hieroglyphs. Many documents survive that reveal just how skilled these artists were:

'I know how to render the posture of a man's statue, the step of a woman's statue, the wing strength of a dozen birds, the bearing of him who strikes a prisoner, the look an eye casts on someone else and also make fearful the face of the sacrificial victim, the arm of him who hits the hippopotamus, the stance of the runner.'

This wall painting from Deir el-Medina shows builders making mud bricks for an Egyptian's tomb.

Source – Mortuary stela of Irtysen, New Kingdom

Words to use in your project

appreciated (*enjoyed*)	**festivities** (*celebrations*)
entertainment (*fun event or activity*)	**income** (*wages*)
	leisure (*free time*)

manual (*done by hand*)
pastime (*hobby*)
supervised (*watched over*)

GAMES

Senet was a popular board game that was even enjoyed by the pharaohs.

Egyptian children loved playing with toys, just as children do today. Many **TOYS** have been found in children's graves, including spinning tops, wooden animals on wheels, colourful clay balls filled with beads or seeds which rattled when they were thrown and dolls made from wood. Board **GAMES** were also popular. In a game called 'senet', players had to try to overcome various dangers to reach the Kingdom of Osiris. We know that even the pharaohs enjoyed playing senet because four senet boards were found in Tutankhamun's tomb. One of the earliest games played in Egypt was called 'the game of snake' because the board was shaped like a coiled serpent. The winner was the first player to reach the snake's head in the centre.

CASE STUDY

MUSIC

Wealthy Egyptians liked to entertain by holding large banquets that included **MUSIC** and **DANCING**. Professional musicians and dancers were hired to entertain the guests while they ate. We know from the paintings found inside tombs that Egyptian musicians played harps, lyres, cymbals and flutes. Tomb inscriptions also tell us about these instruments:

'My majesty made a splendid harp wrought with silver, gold, lapis lazuli, malachite, and every splendid costly stone.'

Many musical instruments have been preserved in tombs. The words to songs were often written on tombs and temple walls.

Harp music was an important part of Egyptian celebrations.

Work and Play Glossary

banquet	A lavish meal or party	**Osiris**	Egyptian god of the dead
constructed	Built or created	**posture**	Way of standing
domestic	Relating to the home	**sacrificial**	Something killed in a ritual
foreman	Worker in charge of others	**scribes**	Professional writers
lyres	Musical instruments with strings	**senet**	A popular board game played in ancient Egypt

Source – Coronation incription of Thutmosis III, c. 1,500 BC

See also: Language and Writing 8–9; Pyramids and Tombs 14–15; Farming 18–19; Families 28–29

Trade and Transport

The River Nile was the main transport route through ancient Egypt. Most people lived near the river and it was the best way to make long JOURNEYS up and down the country. Trade with the land of Nubia was so important that the Egyptians cut a special canal through to Nubia to speed up the journey. They also sailed out further to trade with countries around the Mediterranean Sea.

BUYING AND SELLING

The ancient Egyptians did not use MONEY. Instead, they traded goods for other goods which had the same value. This system was called 'bartering'.

Gold rings are being weighed to see how many deben they are worth in this painting from the tomb of Panekhmen.

Later, a new system was introduced. The value of goods was decided by how many copper weights (or 'deben') an item was worth. One deben was divided into ten smaller weights, called 'kites'. Traders had to obey strict rules or face the wrath of the gods, according to ancient texts:

'Do not move the scales, do not change the weights. He loathes (Re) him who defrauds.'

Egypt was in a good position for trading with other countries in Africa and around the Mediterranean Sea. An example of the EXOTIC GOODS traded is revealed in this inscription:

'... sacks of aromatic gum, gold, ivory, ebony and other valuable woods, leopard skins, live apes, and with natives and their children.'

Sources – The Teachings of Amenemope, Late New Kingdom; and inscription from Hatshepsut's temple at Deir el-Bahiri, c. 1,500 BC

Words to use in your project

cargo *(goods carried by vehicle)*
currency *(local money)*
economy *(wealth of a country)*

exports *(goods sold to other countries)*
expeditions *(journeys)*

imports *(goods bought from other countries)*
saleable *(worth something)*

SHIPS AND BOATS

BOATS were the quickest and easiest way to travel in Egypt and were the main form of transport. The Egyptians were skilled ship-builders. The earliest boats were made from bundles of reeds lashed together. They were used for travelling short distances on hunting or fishing trips. Later, larger boats were made of wood with oars as well as sails. Many model boats have been found in Egyptian tombs. They were put there to provide the dead person with transport in the Next World. Archaeologists have also found a number of actual boats, including one built about 4,500 years ago for King Khufu. The dismantled ship was found buried in a pit next to the Great Pyramid at Giza. Experts reconstructed it to form a royal barge over 40 m long.

Model sailing boats were often placed in tombs to help the dead soul travel to the Next World.

Trade and Transport Glossary

bartering	Trading one item for another	**ebony**	A very valuable type of wood
deben	A copper weight	**lashed**	Fastened securely with cord or rope
defrauds	Gain money by illegal methods	**reconstructed**	Rebuilt or put together again
dismantled	Taken to pieces		

CASE STUDY

Donkeys were used for transporting the harvest.

Donkeys

Wall art and the **DISCOVERY** of many donkey skeletons in a cemetary in Maadi tell us that the Egyptians' main way of travelling on land was by **DONKEY**. They were even used for long trading and mining expeditions. However, the donkey could not survive for long without food and water, so travellers had to take plenty with them, especially when travelling across the hot desert. All peasants kept donkeys, since farming would have been almost impossible to manage without them. Donkeys were also sometimes used to transport the corn to the threshing floor. The horse was not introduced to Egypt until about 1,650 BC.

See also: The Land of Egypt 4–5; Pyramids and Tombs 14–15; Farming 18–19; At Home 26–27

War and Weapons

Although the ancient Egyptians were not particularly war-like, they were quick to FIGHT their enemies in order to expand their empire. Later pharaohs often led military campaigns themselves. Before any campaign, the Egyptians called on the gods to protect the army and help them to defeat their ENEMIES. Scribes accompanied the army into battle, keeping a daily war diary.

THE ARMY

It is estimated that at its height, the Egyptian army was made up of about 100,000 men. It was huge but well organised and highly disciplined. A strict line of command led from the pharaoh down through the generals and officers of different ranks who commanded the units. The army was made of divisions of 5,000 men (4,000 foot-SOLDIERS and 1,000 charioteers). The divisions were named after gods, such as Amun, Ptah and Ra. The long chain of command is clear from this letter:

'Come, [let me tell] you the woes of the soldier, and how many are his superiors: the general, the troop-commander, the officer who leads, the standard-bearer, the lieutenant, the scribe, the commander of fifty, and the garrison-captain.'

Some of the men were professional soliders but others were forced to sign up for major campaigns.

War scenes like the one on this chest were often painted, providing a record of the events that took place on the battlefield.

Source – Instructions of the scribe Nebmare-nakht for his pupil Wenemdiamun Miriam Lichtheim, Late New Kingdom

Words to use in your project

archer *(person who shoots with bow and arrows)*
charioteer *(person who drives chariot)*
combat *(fighting)*
conquer *(win)*
hierarchy *(line of command)*
infantry *(foot soldiers)*
military *(war)*

WEAPONS

Daggers like these from Tutankhamun's tomb would have been used in battle.

Many weapons have been excavated from tombs. They tell us that Egyptian soldiers fought with **SPEARS**, battle-axes, **BOW AND ARROWS** and daggers which were made from wood and bronze. For protection, they carried wooden and leather shields and wore light armour made from leather and bronze. In the New Kingdom, the horse and chariot was introduced which had a big impact on Egyptian warfare.

Egyptian **CHARIOTS** were pulled by two horses and were just big enough for two soldiers to stand in. One soldier drove the chariot while the other attacked the enemy with his bow and arrows or spear. Chariots have only been found in the tombs of pharaohs and the rich because they were very expensive.

War and Weapons Glossary

campaign	The preparations for battle and the battle itself	**rebel**	Going against authority
chariot	Two-wheeled vehicle drawn by horses	**siege**	When a town is surrounded by an enemy army and the people inside cannot get out
divisions	Parts of a whole	**surrendered**	Gave in to let the other side win
garrison	Troops in a fortress		

See also: Pharoahs 6–7; Language and Writing 8–9; Religion 10–11; Work and Play 20–21

CASE STUDY

Pharaoh Tuthmosis III is remembered as Egypt's greatest warrior-king.

The Battle of Megiddo

In 1,457 BC, Pharaoh Tuthmosis III led the Egyptian army against the rebel forces of the Prince of Kadesh in the Battle of Megiddo. He gathered an army of 10,000 men and stormed the city which surrendered after a seige. The whole event was recorded by a scribe whose **BATTLE** report was carved on the walls of the Temple of Karnak, in Thebes:

'All the prInces of all the northern countries are cooped up within it. The capture of Megiddo is the capture of a thousand towns.'

His 17 victorious campaigns made Tuthmosis Egypt's greatest warrior-king.

Source – Inscription from the Amen Temple at Karnak, c. 1,460 BC

At Home

How well an ancient Egyptian lived depended on whether he or she was rich or poor. RICH Egyptians enjoyed luxurious lifestyles, but life was much harder if people were POOR. We know much more about how rich Egyptians lived than ordinary people because the rich left many more objects and buildings behind.

HOUSES

Archaeological remains show that ancient Egyptian HOUSES were built from bricks made from mud from the River Nile.

Wall paintings tell us that they would have been painted white. Windows were small and placed high up to block out the heat and light and keep the houses cool.

This terracotta model of a house, dating from around 1,900 BC, gives us an idea of what kind of houses the Egptian poor lived in.

Wealthy Egyptians had large, spacious houses. Paintings tell us that some also had shady gardens and pools. Inside, the houses were richly decorated with frescoes on the walls and tiles on the floors. Poor Egyptians had much smaller homes, often with only one room in which the whole family lived. Their houses were simply decorated, with little **FURNITURE**. If the land and property were shared amongst a number of people, a list of rights like the one below was drawn up to prevent problems:

'You may go up (to) and down (from) the roof on the stairway of this aforesaid house and you may go in and out (of the front hallway by means of the) main doorway ... and (you) may make any alteration on it ... in proportion to your aforesaid one-eighteenth share ...'.

Source – Bill of sale, Mid-3rd century BC

Words to use in your project

banquet *(feast)*
brewing *(making alcohol)*
consumption *(eating/drinking)*

cookery *(food)*
delicacy *(food treat)*
lavish *(fancy)*

interior *(inside)*
trapping *(catch animal in a trap)*

FOOD AND DRINK

The rich frequently held banquets where many courses of meat, poultry and fruit would be served.

Because of the wide range of crops they grew, the ancient Egyptians ate a variety of **FOODS** which included fruit, vegetables, meat, fish, ducks and geese. Poorer people had simple food, probably consisting of bread, beans, onions and vegetables, with less meat and more fish. Archaeologists rely mainly on wall paintings to work out diet, but a few recipes that were written on ostraca have survived. Beer was very popular to **DRINK**. To make beer, loaves of bread were broken up and mixed with water. The beer was left to ferment, then was strained to get rid of the lumps. One inscription hints at the popularity of the drink:

'*The mouth of a perfectly contented man is filled with beer.*'

Source – Temple inscription, 2,200 BC

At Home Glossary

expedition	*Journey*	**terracotta**	*Brownish-red pottery*
ferment	*Turning to alcohol*	**throwstick**	*A wooden stick, like a boomerang, used for killing birds*
frescoes	*Paintings drawn on plaster*		
luxurious	*Very comfortable and elegant*		
ostraca	*Broken piece of pottery or flake of limestone with writing on it*	**water birds**	*Birds that live near water, such as ducks or swans*

See also: Farming 18–19; Work and Play 20–21; Trade and Transport 22–23; At Home 26–27

CASE STUDY

Hunting and Fishing

As well as growing their own food, the Egyptians also went **HUNTING** and **FISHING**. Many tomb paintings show Egyptians catching fish, birds and animals on the River Nile. Fish were caught in traps, with hooks and lines, or with nets slung between two boats. Larger fish were caught with spears. Water birds were killed by hurling a wooden throwstick at them. Wealthy Egyptians also enjoyed hunting desert animals, such as antelopes, hares and foxes, for sport. Even the kings enjoyed hunting, as proven by accounts such as this one from Pharaoh Amenhotep describing a bull-hunting expedition:

'*There are wild bulls in the desert, in the region of Sheta. His Majesty set out during the night downstream in the royal boat ... [killing] a total of 96 wild bulls.*'

Fishing and hunting were necessary for food but enjoyed as sport as well.

Source – Amenhotep III, c. 1,415 BC

Families

Family life was very important to the ancient Egyptians. CHILDREN were precious and people adopted them if they could not have any of their own. The father was head of the family but women had many rights and privileges that were unusual in the ancient world. Girls as well as boys could inherit their parents' money and property. Old people were well looked after and usually lived with their families where they were greatly respected.

SICKNESS AND HEALTH

Egyptian DOCTORS were highly skilled and well regarded. They may have trained at medical schools, attached to temples.

The best doctors worked in the royal court. Others worked in the community or for the army. By studying the dead bodies of animals, doctors had a good idea of how the body worked and how to treat DISEASES. Some of the treatments listed in ancient texts seem unlikely to have been succesful:

'Diagnosis:– One having a wound above his eyebrow. An ailment which I will treat.

Treatment:– Now after thou hast stitched it, thou shouldst bind fresh meat upon it the first day. If thou findest that the stitching of this wound is loose, thou shouldst ... treat it with grease and honey every day until he recovers.'

Religion was also important. Doctors recited spells and prayers over their patients. Some patients spent a night in the temple in the hope of a miracle cure.

This temple carving shows a selection of medical instruments used by doctors.

28 | Source – The Edwin Smith medical papyrus, probably Old Kingdom in origin

Words to use in your project

compose *(write)*	legal *(to do with the law)*	wife or husband
discipline *(punishment)*	matrimony *(marriage)*	symptom *(sign of a problem)*
education *(learning)*	monogamy *(having only one*	treatment *(medical care)*

LOVE & MARRIAGE

Most **MARRIAGES** were arranged by parents who believed they could identify the best match for their children. Girls from poor families might marry as early as 12 years old. Scribes advised men to treat their wives properly:

'If you take a wife ... she will be attached to you doubly, if her chain is pleasant ... If you are wise, love your wife ... Fill her stomach, clothe her back ... Be not brutal; tact will influence her better than violence.'

If a wife was badly treated, she could divorce her husband. She was then free to marry again if she wanted to. However, most marriages were for life and many couples were even buried in the same grave. Unlike other civilisations of the time, Egyptian men were not allowed more than one wife at a time.

Marriage and family were very important in Egyptian life.

Source – Papyrus Lansing, Late-New Kingdom

CASE STUDY

School

Most Egyptian children did not go to **SCHOOL**. Girls helped their mothers at home, while boys learned their father's trade and began to earn a living. But some children went to schools attached to temples or even to the royal court. These schools were for boys only. They learned how to read and write by copying out and memorising long texts. Later they might go on to higher education and learn how to write legal documents and letters. Most well-educated boys went on to become scribes. If a boy did not listen to his teacher, he might be beaten, as shown in these words of a frustrated teacher to one of his students:

'But though I beat you with every kind of stick, you do not listen. If I knew another way of doing it, I would do it for you, that you might listen.'

Only a small number of children went to school. They learnt to read and write by copying texts like this one.

Families Glossary

ailment	A minor illness		when they die
divorce	When a marriage breaks down and a couple splits up	memorising	Learning off by heart
		privileges	Special rights
inherit	To be given a person's money and property	tact	Careful handling
		text	Something written down

See also: Language and Writing 8–9; Religion 10–11; Work and Play 20–21; At Home 26–27

Source – The Precepts of Ptoh-Hotep, 2,200 BC

Clothes and Jewellery

Ancient Egyptians, both rich and poor, seem to have taken a great deal of care over their appearance. Since Egyptian FASHION changed very slowly over hundreds of years, people did not have lots of new looks and styles to try out. Instead, they took pride in keeping themselves and their clothes neat and clean. Both men and women liked to wear make-up and jewellery, and many beautiful pieces of jewellery have been found in Egyptian tombs.

CLOTHES

We know what the ancient Egyptians wore from the many illustrations of people in tomb paintings that have survived.

Because of the hot climate, most Egyptian clothes were light and loose fitting. Clothes were all made from **LINEN**. For a man, the basic costume was a practical linen loin cloth or a simple kilt, wrapped around the waist and tied with a knot. Women wore long, tunic-style **DRESSES**. Cloaks or shawls were sometimes worn on top. On their feet, people wore simple **SANDALS** made from papyrus reeds. It was usual, though, for people to go barefoot and carry their sandals, putting them on when it was necessary.

This painting of a middle-class man and woman dressed in finely pleated white linen robes is from a tomb at Deir el-Medina.

JEWELLERY

Wide collars made of many roman beads were popular throughout Egyptian history.

Archaeological evidence suggests that rich and poor Egyptians of both sexes liked to wear jewellery. Poorer people wore rings, **NECKLACES** and earrings made from cheaper metals, such as copper, decorated with coloured stones and glazes. But wealthy Egyptians had a choice of gold and silver, inlaid with glass or semi-precious stones, such as red carnelian, deep blue lapis lazuli and light blue turquoise. Egyptian jewellers became experts at working these into beautiful necklaces, pendants, bracelets, earrings, anklets and rings. Many pieces of jewellery included sacred symbols, worn as **LUCKY CHARMS**. Tutankhamun's tomb contained a magnificent collection of jewellery revealing the wealth of the pharaohs and the skill of their jewellers.

CASE STUDY

Hair and Make-up

Egyptian art tells us that most men and women wore their **HAIR** cut short which was more comfortable in the warm weather. But on special occasions, such as banquets and official functions, wealthier people liked to wear black wigs made from wool or human hair. **MAKE-UP** was also widely used. Both men and women used black eyepaint, called kohl, to line their eyes. Lips and cheeks were painted red with powered ochre. Cosmetics were often kept in highly decorated or carved containers. Mirrors were made from polished copper or bronze, not from glass.

Make-up was stored in coloured containers like these ones found in various tombs.

Clothes and Jewellery Glossary

cosmetics	Make-up, perfumes and other beauty products	ochre	A type of clay
		papyrus	Type of reed plant used to make many things
inlaid	Objects placed firmly somewhere for decoration	pendants	Type of necklace
kilt	A short, skirt-like garment	tunic	Long sleeveless garment reaching the thighs or knees
kohl	Black eyeliner		
linen	Cloth woven from fibres from the flax plant		

See also: Pyramids and Tombs 14–15; Trade and Transport 22–23; At Home 26–27; Families 28–29

Index

ANCIENT EGYPT TIMELINE

About 5,000 BC
The strip of land by the River Nile becomes known as Lower Egypt (northern part) and Upper Egypt (southern part).

About 3,100 BC
Lower and Upper Egypt are united under one ruler, called Menes.

2,686–2,181 BC
Old Kingdom

2,680 BC
Egypt's first pyramid is built at Saqqara.

About 2,580 BC
The Great Pyramid at Giza is completed.

2,181–2,055 BC
First Intermediate Period

2,055–1,650 BC
Middle Kingdom

2,055 BC
Upper and Lower Egypt are reunited by Mentuhotep II. The first great temples are built at Karnak.

1,650–1,550 BC
*Second Intermediate Period
The Hyksos invade from Palestine and nearby, and conquer Lower Egypt.*

1,550–1,069 BC
New Kingdom

1,550 BC
The Hyksos are driven out of Egypt.

1,504–1,492 BC
Pharaoh Tuthmosis I reigns. He is the first Egyptian ruler to have a rock-cut tomb in the Valley of the Kings.

1,352–1,336 BC
Pharaoh Akhenaten rules Egypt.

1,336–1,327 BC
Tutankhamun is pharaoh.

1,279–1,213 BC
Ramesses II rules Egypt. The temple at Abu Simbel is built.

1,184–1,153 BC
Rameses III reigns.

1,069–747 BC
Third Intermediate Period

747–332 BC
Late Period

525–404 BC
Persia invades and takes control of Egypt. After the Persians are defeated, the country returns to Egyptian rule.

About 450 BC
The Greek traveller and historian Herodotus visits Egypt.

323 BC–AD 395
Greek-Roman Period

343–332 BC
Persia invades again, and regains control of Egypt.

332 BC
The Persians are overthrown by the armies of Alexander the Great. Egypt becomes part of his Greek Empire.

196 BC
The Rosetta Stone is carved.

51–30 BC
Cleopatra VII, rules. Egypt is conquered by the Romans and becomes part of the Roman Empire.